SELF-DEFENSE

GOODYEAR PHYSICAL ACTIVITIES SERIES
EDITED BY J. TILLMAN HALL

SELF-DEFENSE

LYNN M. PACALA

Goodyear Publishing Company, Inc.
Santa Monica, California 90401

Library of Congress Cataloging in Publication Data

Pacala, Lynn M
  Self-Defense

  (Goodyear physical activities series)
  Bibliography: p. 105
  1. Self-defense.   I. Title.
GV1111.P25   613.6'6   80-14488
ISBN 0-8302-8204-1

SELF-DEFENSE
Lynn M. Pacala
Copyright © 1980 by
GOODYEAR PUBLISHING COMPANY, INC.
Santa Monica, California 90401
Current printing (last digit):
10 9 8 7 6 5 4 3 2 1
Y-8204-3
Printed in the United States of America

ACKNOWLEDGMENTS

I wish to thank the following individuals and group who made this book possible: Shihan Takiyuki Kubota, for years of training in developing awareness of the various components of the martial arts; *Women in Martial Arts*, for hours of discussion relating to the effectiveness of self-defense training; Dr. J. Tillman Hall, who encouraged me to write this book; my husband, Thomas, who supported me during its writing. I also wish to thank the models for the pictures: Mr. Jim Barker, Ms. Juanita Dotson, Mr. Ron Higuera, Dr. Robert Hopper, Mr. Dennis Jablonski, Mr. Colby Parks, Mr. Greg Pickrel, Mr. Gary Smith, Mr. John Sweet and Ms. Ellen Tirone.

CONTENTS

BIOGRAPHY

Lynn Marevich Pacala is Assistant Professor of Physical Education at Occidental College. She received her B.S., M.S., and Ph.D. from the University of Southern California. Since 1973, Pacala has trained with Master Takiyuki Kubota, and holds a second degree black belt in Shotokan karate. In addition to designing and teaching self-defense courses and lecture demonstrations, Pacala has written several articles on the subject, and sits on the Board of Directors of *Women in Martial Arts*.

EDITOR'S NOTE

Self-Defense is a timely addition to the Goodyear Physical Activities Series. The author, Dr. Lynn M. Pacala, is a uniquely qualified authority on the subject: she holds a second-degree black belt in Shotokan karate, teaches self-defense courses and gives demonstrations, writes articles on the subject, and is a member of the Board of Directors of *Women in Martial Arts*.

This book is for the ordinary person who wants to understand the basic principles of defending him or herself from attack. It is written in a direct, "DO THIS" style with over 100 photos that show the reader "HOW." Throughout the book a problem is described and alternative defensive actions (with advantages and disadvantages of each indicated) are illustrated.

Pacala stresses that the best self-defense is to avoid trouble and shows you how to assess your awareness. She tells you how to refine your natural instincts into conscious, effective, defensive reactions. She reminds you of the basic tenets of personal safety at home, work, school, travel; and points out the defensive arsenal you usually have with you (your purse, briefcase, books, clothes, head, hands, arms, feet, elbows, and knees).

In the *Basic Skills* section you'll learn the fundamentals of self-defense: beginning with stance and progressing through the use of your feet, legs, hands, fingers, and elbows as defensive weapons. Protective movements and releases are treated with the same detail as the basic skills.

A special discussion of how to handle yourself when you are disadvantaged (called *Losing the First Round*) presents information usually omitted in self-defense teaching. To help you "keep in shape," Lynn Pacala wraps up this practical self-help book with a fitness and practice section. The *Performance Checklists* and self-tests in the back of the book will help you gauge your progress.

WHAT IS SELF-DEFENSE?

Today we are faced with increasing crime against individuals as well as their property. This increase has created a growing concern for self-protection. Individuals in today's society need to feel secure, live comfortably, and interact with others in a compatible manner. When the harmony of interpersonal relations is jarred, individuals need to compensate and act accordingly.

In the past few years self-defense courses, texts and articles have received notoriety due to their focus— teaching people how to protect themselves. Self-defense instruction provides individuals with a means of regaining comfort and confidence at home, as well as in positive and negative interactions with others.

For the purpose of this book, self-defense is defined as defense of self: not your mother, brother or aunt but *YOU*. Although most of the basic skills presented in this text can be applied to the defense of others, the main focus will be on you—on providing you with enough information to handle yourself in a stressful situation.

1

DIMENSIONS OF SELF-DEFENSE

The question of whether or not there is value in self-defense is an appropriate one. Some people believe that self-defense courses provide a false sense of security, resulting in students who believe they can protect themselves in any possible situation, when in reality they do not possess the needed abilities. Self-defense has three interdependent dimensions: (1) the psychological, (2) the cognitive, and (3) the physical. It is through the development of these dimensions that the individual attains an adequate means of self-protection.

The Psychological Dimension

The psychological dimension is the individual's emotional ability to deal with a threatening situation; the most important aspect of which is the individual's mental preparedness to recognize and avoid situations which could lead to danger. This awareness can be referred to as the "common-sense" aspect of self-defense awareness. Psychological readiness is the ability to analyze a situation and respond in an appropriate manner. If physical contact or threat of physical violence occurs, you must have the psychological confidence to take charge of the situation by responding quickly and effectively.

Many people have difficulty in matching intent with force. The intent of the assailant is the actual or perceived act, while force is the tactic or the amount of power needed to defend the act. As with most behaviors, you need to believe that you are in danger before you can react. Someone rehearsed in self-defense skills must believe that the assailant *does* mean him harm, and thereby can behave accordingly. *An assailant who attacks you should not be left slightly hurt but rather incapacitated.* You need to develop the ability to match intent with force.

The Cognitive Dimension

The second dimension of self-defense deals with the cognitive process. That is, the understanding of the skills involved in protecting yourself and the ramifications of possessing those skills. This book will explain the principles involved in the execution of certain skilled movements with emphasis placed on the implications of particular moves. It will also examine the commonalities of certain types of movements. Since instances requiring self-defense measures are situational, this cognitive knowledge must be synthesized with the psychological and physical dimensions to be effective in various self-defense situations.

The Physical Dimension

The physical dimension refers to skill attainment. Each individual needs to acquire the skill proficiency level necessary to carry out self-defense. The physical dimension applies to the ability to move efficiently and effectively. Therefore, the practice of learned skills is necessary. Although self-defense is not a sport per se, the amount of practice or rehearsal time necessary to increase proficiency is analogous. The fundamental movements such as striking, kicking and running must be practiced. The optimal skill level reached will differ from individual to individual and is contingent upon two variables: (1) the individual's overall skill level, and (2) the amount of practice time put into the skills. The second variable is one which you have control over. As with most skills, practice increases the level of proficiency; and physical practice is one thing that no one can do for another.

AWARENESS

Developing self-defense awareness is not something which is automatically developed by taking a course or reading a book; however, these are means which provide a basis for understanding and, more importantly, provide individuals with a realistic view of how this awareness can be developed.

Self-defense awareness implies the ability to be cognizant of threatening situations or environments. In day to day situations you have the choice of entering a possibly threatening situation or avoiding it. Think of how many times you may have walked down a deserted street because it was closer to your destination, or driven at night with your car door unlocked, or accepted an invitation with someone who seemed like a nice person. These are but a few of the common situations which we all face daily. Self-defense consciousness becomes the awareness to recognize environments and evaluate the possible repercussions of any choice. The choice then becomes whether or not to interact in a certain environment.

NATURAL VERSUS LEARNED RESPONSES

Preferential Movements

Each of you possess certain movement patterns which, through repetition, have become automatic or reflexive. These movements require no conscious thought process. For example, if a heavy object is hurtled toward you, more often than not you will do one of two things: either dodge the object or attempt to block the object to avoid injury. Either response is automatic, depending upon the individual. Everyone has a variety of dominant movement patterns. The choice of whether to dodge the object with the whole body, or to block it with the arm, shows a movement preference. Adult movement preferences are the sum total of previous experiences. Frequently repeated movements become automatic over a period of time; while infrequently repeated movements are generally less efficient and demand more conscious effort in their execution. Movements which require a conscious effort are not spontaneous in nature.

Knowing Your Preferences . . .
Recognize and Refine

In an unpredicted spontaneous attack, the victim has a minimal amount of "thinking" time, therefore reflexive movements and reactions are a necessity. Since you have established preferential movement patterns, you need to (1) *recognize movements which feel natural or reflexive*, and (2) *refine those natural movements to such an extent that they become highly effective when called upon in a defensive situation.*

Increasing your movement repertoire means progressing through a learning process. As you begin to understand the movement in conjunction with the physical rehearsal of the movement, less conscious effort is required to execute the movement. Finally, an automatic stage, where no conscious effort is required to execute the movement, is reached. The following example illustrates this point. A professional basketball player is passed the ball and begins to dribble down the court, preparing to shoot. Although he is consciously aware that other players are trying to guard him he continues to dribble the ball. The actual movements involved in dribbling the ball are unconscious in nature to this professional player. On the other hand, the novice player who has not rehearsed this dribbling movement to the degree of the professional must exert a conscious effort to keep on dribbling the ball. The more movements are practiced over a period of time, the more spontaneous the movements in your movement repertoire become. The black belt in karate has spent years learning and refining movements used in self-defense. In many instances the expert has reached this level where no conscious effort is required to execute a defense. It is not until the individual reaches this unconscious effort level that the movement becomes natural to that individual.

Since most people interested in self-defense do not intend to spend years becoming a karate expert, some type of short-cut method is needed. Since everyone has movement preferences, effective defensive measures can be attained by refining these pre-established preferences. Someone with a tendency to swing the arm out has excellent potential for developing this swinging motion into a "backhand" motion—a highly effective attack. In this motion the back portion of the hand (the knuckles) is used. Likewise, people who tend to "nudge" others with their elbow can more easily refine this "nudge" into an elbow attack than learn a new movement to take its place. Here the elbow is used as the striking implement. The bony structure of the elbow plus the power of the "nudge" is quite forceful. It therefore becomes increasingly important to recognize your preferential movements and to refine them.

2

PERSONAL SAFETY

THE INDIVIDUAL'S RESPONSIBILITY

Each one of you has a responsibility for your own safety. In many instances someone has become the "victim" due to failure to accept this responsibility. Personal responsibility is the willingness to assess yourself in situations, make choices of how to deal with them, and accept the ramifications of those choices. When becoming self-defense conscious you must become aware of choices and repercussions. This chapter presents the precautions you should take at home and when traveling. The choice to take them is up to you. Through these precautions you will become self-defense conscious by recognizing danger and eliminating or avoiding it.

HOME PRECAUTIONS

When at home the following precautions should be taken to lessen the possibility of becoming a "victim."

- Always secure proper identification before opening your door. Repair people (i.e. telephone, gas) must carry identification with them at all times. Don't be afraid to ask for identification and especially don't be afraid to refuse entry when identification is suspicious.

- Install a peephole in order to view visitors.

- If living in an apartment, list your name on the directory or mailbox with only your last name, or first initial and last name.

- If living in a security apartment complex, never "buzz in" individuals without first having them identify themselves—even if you are expecting someone.

- When entering a garage with a security gate system, avoid letting another car in with you.

- When moving into a new apartment or house, change the locks throughout. You never know who may have duplicates of the old keys.

- Avoid making duplicate keys for "friends"; circumstances can change.

- Keep blinds and curtains closed at night.

- If living alone, avoid broadcasting this fact.

- Install additional lock on door when only a standard key lock is present. Deadbolt locks are the most secure.

Phone Precautions

The following precautions may minimize possible victimization.

- List your phone number using your first initial and last name rather than your entire name.

- Unlisted phone numbers are inexpensive and worth the investment.

- If you live alone or happen to be by yourself, don't provide this information to strangers.

- If you receive a wrong number do not give out your number as a correction.

- Hang up immediately on an obscene phone call.

- If an obscene caller persists, blow a whistle into the receiver or tap lightly into the receiver with a pencil and say something like "Officer, this is the person I called you about."

TRAVELING PRECAUTIONS

Observe the following precautions when traveling.

Walking

- Walk with confidence. Always keep a brisk pace. If you see a suspicious character in your path, cross the street.

- Always walk in well-lighted areas.

- Stay away from dark buildings and alleys. They are excellent hiding places for assailants.

- Learn to recognize when you are being followed. Change your walking pace. If the individual following you changes his, it's time to seek aid.

- Your clothing may be perceived as expressing vulnerability. Avoid wearing suggestive clothing.

- A large briefcase or purse swinging from your hand attracts attention. Keep the briefcase or purse clutched or tucked under your arm.

- When traveling to your home, apartment or car, always have the correct key in your hand. Not only can it be used as a weapon but this precaution prevents the lapse of time trying to locate it at your destination.

Car

- Always check the back seat of your car before entering. Many assailants have used this as a hiding place to surprise their victims.

- Keep your windows rolled up at night. When driving, your doors should always be kept locked.
- Always park in well-lighted areas.
- Never stop to help a stranded motorist; call for help from the nearest phone. Give an accurate location of the motorist.
- If you have car trouble, avoid accepting a ride to the gas station. Ask the helpful motorist to seek aid for you.
- If your safety is threatened while at a stoplight or parked, blast your horn and leave as quickly as possible.
- Avoid traveling to new places at night, particularly if unfamiliar with the area or if you are traveling alone.
- If stopped by a law enforcement officer in an unmarked car, ask for identification before rolling down the car window.
- When leaving your car with valet parking or to be serviced, leave only the car keys. Take your other keys with you.

Bus

- Avoid falling asleep when riding a bus.
- Avoid entering into personal conversations with individuals you may meet.
- Don't be afraid to move or to inform the bus driver when being annoyed by another passenger.

Elevator

- If you are riding alone in an elevator and a suspicious character enters, exit immediately.

Hitchhiking

A hitchhiker generally takes responsibility for whatever may happen. Again, hitchhikers make a choice when deciding to use this mode of transportation. Suggested precautions are as follows:

- Never accept a ride from someone who has changed directions to accommodate you.

- Never allow yourself to be sandwiched between two individuals when riding.

- When you accept a ride, always sit near the door, keeping it unlocked with your belongings next to it.

- Always keep your hand on the door to make ready for a speedy exit.

COMMON WEAPONS

Many commonly carried items can be used as effective weapons. Examples of these are keys, umbrellas, pens, a briefcase, and so forth.

Figure 2.1
The key should be held firmly between the thumb and forefinger.

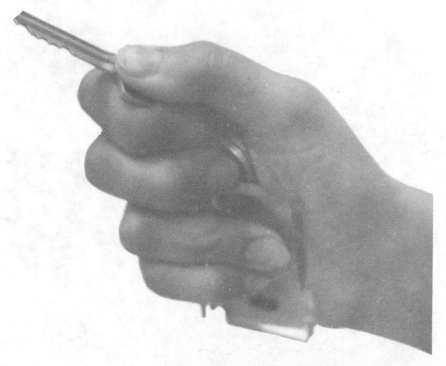

It is very important to realize that any item used *by* an individual as a weapon can be used *against* the individual as a weapon. The self-defense conscious person is aware of this fact and only uses weapons when confident of their usage. Generally these weapons should be used only to provide an opportunity to flee. Items such as keys and pencils should be used to strike to vulnerable areas, particularly the face. By jabbing or puncturing the assailant a two-fold purpose is met: (1) deterring the assailant and providing time to flee, and

Figure 2.2
A key can be used to scratch or puncture the face.

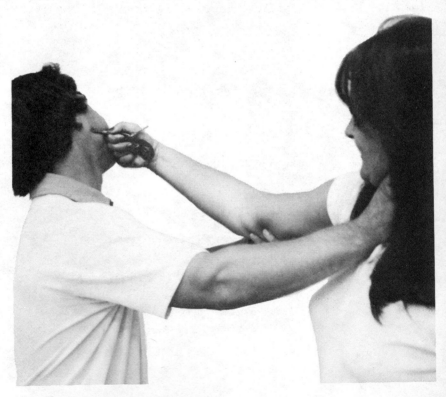

Figure 2.3
A ballpoint pen is used to puncture the hand.

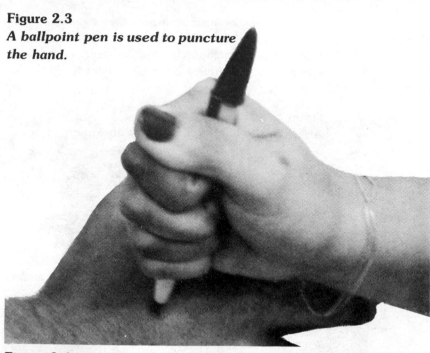

Figure 2.4
A textbook is shoved into the throat.

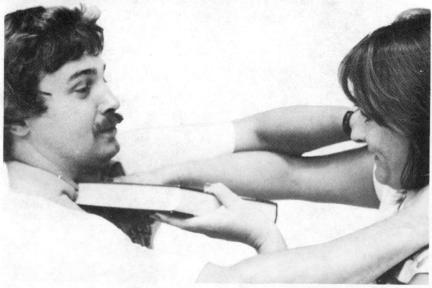

(2) leaving an identifiable mark on the assailant. Although any injury will, to a lesser or greater degree, deter the assailant, the facial area is almost always exposed and extremely vulnerable to pain.

Figure 2.5
An umbrella is thrust into the abdomen.

REPORTING AN ASSAULT

Every attempted assault should be reported to the police immediately. The police are usually very cooperative in aiding the individual. The length of time from when the call is placed and when the police arrive varies. An assault in progress takes precedence over one which has occurred, or an attempted assault.

When the officers arrive you will be asked to describe the assailant and the assault in detail. If witnesses were present they are usually interviewed individually since the stress of an assault often causes conflicting stories. The assailant's jacket—which appeared brown to one individual—may have looked black to another. The officers are not doubting the validity of anyone's account of the incident, but rather realize that frequently those involved are under stress and confused. Sometimes people remember details of the incident at a later time. This additional information should be reported to the police. The investigating officers will ask you specific questions regarding the assailant. The self-defense conscious person must be observant of any distinguishing characteristic, whether it be a speech or walking pattern, or any other physical feature of the assailant, or would-be assailant. Although the clothes of the assailant are important, they are temporary in nature. It is far easier to change your clothes than to change your appearance. The police request the following information on all assailants:

- sex
- ethnic descent
- hair color
- eye color
- height
- weight

- age
- type of clothing
- name and address (if known)
- personal oddities (unusual features, scars, tattoos, etc.)
- weapon.

If the assailant left the scene in a vehicle the officers will ask questions regarding the car's make and model, color, license number, and condition of the car.

MEDICAL ATTENTION

Procedures for cases requiring medical attention vary from area to area. For instance, in Los Angeles if an ambulance is needed, the police are authorized to call the nearest emergency hospital. You have the option of seeking medical aid of your own. Victims are issued a slip identifying them as victims of a violent crime. The slip will have a *report number* and list the reporting officer's name. This number should be used when referring to, or providing any additional information pertaining to the incident.

The severity of the assault generally dictates what type of medical attention is needed. If any type of strikes or blows transpired during the assault you should see your physician, even if you appear to feel fine. Most assaults produce a degree of shock so that you may not be aware of the extent of your injuries.

RAPE

Rape is classified as a violent crime. Although situations differ, the would-be victim must try to size up the psychological framework of the rapist. When rape is imminent, the would-be victim must select a strategy based upon the interplay of the following variables: the psychological framework of the individual; the perceived framework of the assailant; and the particular situation. Three options will be discussed. The first option is one of stalling, bargaining for time by talking to the rapist. Since rape is a violent crime, psychologists have suggested that the rapist enjoys the violence associated with rape rather than the specific sexual act. Avoid pleading for mercy.

The second option is resisting and counterattacking. If you choose this option you must realize that once you attack, you commit yourself. You may very well be fighting for your life. Reports show that half-hearted resistance measures only lead to more violence in the act.

The third option is submission. Concentrate on the rapist's M.O. (mode of operation) and on remembering as many details as possible—this may ultimately lead to the rapist's capture.

Reporting a Rape

All rapes should be reported to the police immediately. Although most rape victims have expressed a strong desire to bathe immediately and, in a sense, wash themselves clean of the act, *don't.* You will be removing important evidence. Do not bathe or remove your clothing. When the police arrive they will take your statement as they would any other report. Give details regarding what the rapist said and did. The shock factor in rape cases often makes follow-up visits for additional information necessary.

Rape victims are either met at the hospital by the police, or the report is taken at the scene. Following the report you will be examined by a physician for cuts and bruises; skin and blood traces may be taken from behind the fingernails; and semen smears will be taken from areas of entry. All of these specimens are necessary and can ultimately lead to the capture of the rapist. During the examination a police officer is present; however, a female officer may be requested. Bruises and cuts may be photographed at the time of examination in order to substantiate the medical report.

THE BODY AS A WEAPON

When developing self-defense consciousness, you must view yourself as more than a potential victim. The human body is multidimensional in its use—it can be injured, cause injury, or prevent injury.

Every body carries with it certain weapons which you must be aware of and expand to their fullest potential. First, these weapons must be identified and developed. Second, each of you must identify your most natural movements and work to refine them. In doing so, the body weapons used in those movements will become more reliable.

THE BODY'S WEAPONS

Three body parts emerge as potential body weapons. They are the head, the hands, and the feet.

Head

The use of the head in defense is two-fold. First, the head can set the psychological advantage. As a self-defense conscious individual, you must analyze the situation and respond effectively to it; matching strategy with intent. Secondly, a subsystem of the head is the vocal system or voice. The ability to scream acts as a defense because it can elicit aid and possibly frighten the assailant. Scream as loudly as possible.

Figure 3.1
The body weapons.

Hands

The hands can deliver blows which can seriously injure an assailant. Among these blows are punches, palm attacks, backhands, ridgehands. (See Chapter 8.) Other hand attacks are finger attacks, such as gouging, scratching and pulling.

Feet

The feet are considered weapons for two reasons. First, they provide a mode of transportation—running. Running away from a threatening situation defeats the expectations of the assailant. The second use of the feet as weapons lies in the ability to kick. Kicks can generate enough power to incapacitate the assailant.

VITAL TARGET AREAS

Certain areas of the body are vulnerable. A properly executed attack to one of these areas can incapacitate the assailant. A knowledge of these areas is desirable for two purposes. First, it provides the individual with targets to aim at when counterattacking. Second, it makes the individual aware of the vital areas which should be protected from an assailant.

The following six areas are vulnerable.

Eyes

An attack to the eyes usually causes enough pain to force the assailant to relinquish any hold or terminate the attack. Pain to the eyes disturbs both vision and equilibrium.

Nose

An attack to the nose generally causes a great deal of pain and interfers with vision.

Throat

Attacks to the throat area cause constriction in the throat; thereby interfering with the swallowing process and, ultimately, the breathing process.

Solar Plexus

The solar plexus is located midway between the chest and abdomen. Attacks to this area will cause the assailant to become "winded." Severe blows can cause unconsciousness.

Groin

The groin is an extremely sensitive area for all men. Attacks to this area always cause severe pain. If you choose an attack to the groin the blow must be severe. A weak attack can infuriate an attacker.

Knees

From a structural standpoint, the inside and the outside of the knee cap is extremely weak. A well-delivered kick can incapacitate an assailant by tearing cartilage in the area. An assailant who cannot walk cannot pursue you.

Figure 3.2
The vital target areas.

BASIC SKILLS

Efficient use of movement is the key to power. The ability to execute a movement with efficient and confident form enables the would-be victim to take an offensive position. Each of you has certain movements which are more natural than others. It is up to you to refine these natural movements to maximize their efficiency.

SPONTANEOUS AND DELAYED ATTACKS

Although each encounter is different, there are certain commonalities which all assaults share, whether they are spontaneous attacks or delayed attacks. Spontaneous attacks are those which occur without any forewarning. In delayed assaults there is a time-lapse from the initial victim-assailant encounter to the actual assault. Both types of confrontations are stressful as well as frightening.

The second type of attack allows the would-be victim time to "size up" the situation. A precise thought-pattern in conjunction with effective movements may determine success or failure.

INGRAINED MOVEMENT PATTERNS

Spontaneous attacks require prompt and accurate movements. Spontaneous defensive and offensive movements are those which are most often rehearsed. A movement pattern becomes ingrained in your movement repertoire through rehearsal or repetition.

In watching young children play you will observe that some tend to be leg dominant. Most of their play, as well as their aggressive behavior, revolves around the use of their legs (i.e. kicking). Others tend to be arm or hand dominated and most of their behavior is manifest in arm and hand movements (i.e. striking). Adult behavior parallels this. If two people were given a hearty shove from behind without warning, each would probably respond differently. Perhaps one would turn around with a hand raised, while the other might prepare to kick. Individuals tend to revert to frequently rehearsed movements in stressful situations. Therefore, if you have rehearsed more hand or striking motions and you are taken by surprise, you will instinctively rely on a striking defense. Likewise, if you have had more experience in kicking, a kick will be your first move.

Chapters 4, 5, 6 and 7 give you information about the most efficient way to execute the various defense movements. Every movement will not feel natural to you. They are presented so that you have as many alternatives for defensive and offensive movements as possible. You are responsible for choosing the movements that fit you. When determining which movements are best for you, consider the following factors: (1) the nature of the movement (the type and quality of the movement), (2) the naturalness of the movement (the ease with which the movement can be unconsciously executed), (3) your physical ability versus your assailant's ability, and (4) your awareness of the mechanics of the movements in terms of potential.

No Rules

It should be noted that as there are no rules to guide you in defending yourself—ANYTHING GOES! If kicking or screaming or spitting are comfortable for you . . . USE THEM! Remember that the assailant will use all of *his* assets in assaulting *you*.

STANCE

A strong stance can demonstrate a certain degree of offensiveness. Whoever sets the tone has the advantage in any given situation. In a possible attack situation, the assailant (by his or her presence), has probably already set the tone. Mental preparedness allows the would-be victim to turn the tables on the assailant. A confident stance can help you achieve this. Your first reaction, after the initial surprise, may telegraph to your assailant whether or not you will be his next victim. A strong stance can easily say to your assailant, "Hey, I'm not intimidated!"

The suggested stance is one in which one foot is slightly in front of the other, with both knees slightly flexed and weight distributed slightly forward on the toes. This stance aids you in maintaining balance. The arms should be flexed about waist height with the hands in front. Generally, the dominant hand should be slightly drawn back for a quick hand attack if necessary. Having one foot back will accommodate hip rotation; an added source of power to any leg or arm attack. The arms and hands in this position can quickly and easily either block or strike the assailant. This stance also allows less body area to be exposed. No one can attack what is not there.

Make direct eye contact with the assailant. This can give you a psychological edge and may help you identify the assailant at a later time. The calmer and more confident you portray yourself to be, the better. Any edge, whether it be psychological or physical, is important.

Figure 3.3
In this stance one foot is slightly forward with both knees flexed and weight distributed slightly forward on the toes.

USE OF THE FEET

RUNNING

Due to the unpredictability of assaults and the
environments surrounding them, running may or may
not be a viable solution. If there is a short distance
to safety, then running may be the answer. While
running scream loudly, drawing as much attention to
yourself as possible. Conversely, if there is no indication
of how far you may have to run to seek aid and safety,
running may be nothing more than a waste of energy.
Men can usually run longer distances than women.
Consider the following points when determining whether
or not to run: the amount of energy you will use in
running and screaming, your overall physical condition,
and the distance to be covered. In some instances it may
be self-defeating to use up all of your energy running
and then have to defend yourself against an angry
assailant.

KICKS

The combination of the leg with hip thrust creates the most powerful unit of the body. Because the legs are the longest single segment of the body, they enable you to simultaneously strike and keep the assailant at bay. The reach potential in conjunction with power potential makes the kick one of the most useful attacks available to you. To increase the possibility of disabling the assailant a kick should be combined with hand techniques whenever possible.

The kicks presented in the following pages include: the front kick, the side kick, and the stomping kick. Each of these will be presented separately. However, they have commonalities as follows.

Figure 4.1
The reach of a kick exceeds that of a punch.

Figure 4.2
The center of gravity falls outside the supporting leg.

Incorrect

Correct

Figure 4.3
The center of gravity should fall within the base of the supporting leg.

The source of power in kick delivery is the hip. In all kicks the center of gravity should fall within the base area of the supporting foot. If this does not occur, balance and power will degenerate. Individuals generally prefer to kick with their dominant leg. Individuals generally develop leg preference along with hand dominance. The dominant leg is stronger and most easily controlled. In practicing kicks, make a mental note of which leg seems to be stronger and more coordinated.

Front Kick

The front kick is used when being approached from the front. The two dominant target areas are 1) the groin, and 2) the inside or outside of the knee. Kicks going higher than these levels can easily be caught unless a great deal of time is spent in developing quick timing.

Contact is made with the ball of the foot when executing a front kick. Kicking and making contact with the toes pointed is a good way to injure them. The ball of the foot should be thrust forward with the toes pulled back. If shoes are worn the contact point remains the same. The various types of footwear yield different advantages: thick soled shoes or boots give a weighted delivery, while running shoes allow for well-controlled thrust since the soles are pliable. Experiment with different types of shoes with the ball of the foot extended. Kicking a padded wall is a good way to see where contact would be made.

Figure 4.4
The ball of the foot is the contact area when executing the front kick.

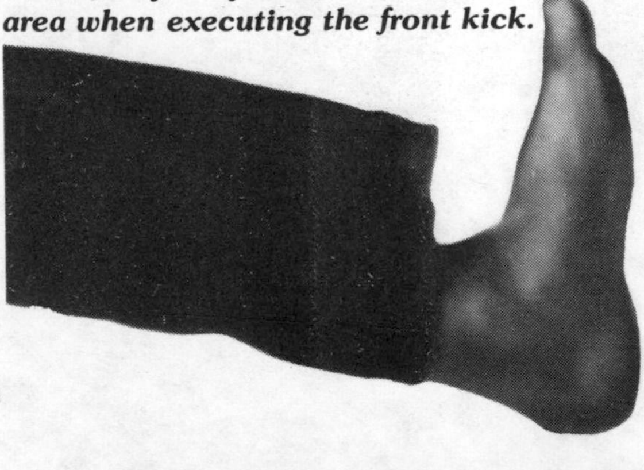

To deliver a front kick:

1. Assume a stance position.

2. Raise the knee of the kicking leg in order to gain height when executing the kick.

3. Keep the supporting leg flexed for balance, with weight distributed equally between the toes and heel.

4. Keep the lower portion of the kicking leg as close to the upper portion of the leg as possible.

5. Tense the muscles in the ankle as the heel is drawn back, causing the ball of the foot to be extended.

6. Extend the leg fully in a snapping motion to the target area, using the hips for thrust.

7. Withdraw the kicking leg.

8. Return to stance.

Figure 4.5
Progression of the front kick.

Side Kick

The side kick is executed in much the same manner as the front kick, with the following exceptions. The side kick is utilized in kicking to the side of the body. The contact area of the foot is the outside edge of the foot toward the heel. The trajectory of the kick maximizes the power in this contact location. Like the front kick, the target areas are 1) the groin and, 2) the inside and outside of the knee.

Figure 4.6
Contact is made with the side of the foot when executing the side kick.

To execute the side kick:

1. Raise the knee, tilting the edge of the kicking foot parallel with the floor.

2. Make sure the toes of the kicking foot face forward; thus exerting tension in the ankle and slightly extending the heel.

3. Keep the supporting leg bent with the weight distributed equally from toe to heel.

4. Extend the leg to the target area in a snapping motion.

5. Withdraw the leg quickly.

Figure 4.7
The progression of the side kick.

Figure 4.8
Progression of the stomping kick.

Stomping Kick

The stomping kick is the only kick where the weight is transferred onto the kick leg. The stomping kick is accurately described by its name. The intent behind a stomping kick is to make contact with the assailant's instep (top of the foot), with your heel, which is extended downward. The trajectory of the downward stomping action maximizes the power of the heel contact. A forceful stomping kick can disable the assailant. An assailant with an injured instep is unlikely to be able to pursue you.

A stomping kick is used at close range. In a close range attack and counterattack, it should be emphasized that the assailant has dictated the close proximity. Keeping distance when you have control of the situation is of key importance.

In executing a stomping kick the following motions should be executed:

1. Raise the knee of the kicking leg as high as possible while keeping the supporting leg slightly flexed for balance.

2. Thrust the heel of the foot down onto the instep of the assailant.

3. Straighten the supporting leg and transfer weight onto the kicking leg as the heel is thrust onto the assailant's instep.

Note: When practicing this kick use padded mat or avoid transferring weight fully as injury to heel may occur.

5

USE OF HANDS AND ELBOWS

Hands and elbows can be effective weapons when used efficiently. These two body parts usually have been conditioned to fit the individual's pre-established movement preference. Some people find making contact with a fisted hand unnatural, and that using the back of the knuckles in a slapping motion is natural. The fisted hand may become a learned response for these people. In instances of high stress, learned responses probably will not be the first response, instead a natural response will probably be used.

The distance that the arm, hand and elbow can reach is limited compared to the maximum distance of a kick. Hand and elbow attacks should only be used when there is close proximity between the individual and the assailant. Trying to obtain greater distance in a hand attack by leaning with it will only result in loss of power and balance.

The following hand and elbow attacks will be discussed in this chapter: striking with a fist; palm attacks; backhand attacks; gouging, scratching, pulling and jabs; and back, side, and front elbow strikes.

HAND ATTACKS

Most hand attacks have a common target area. Generally, hand attacks are used to strike to the facial area: the eyes, nose and throat all being extremely vulnerable and unprotected. The solar plexus is also a prime choice for attack.

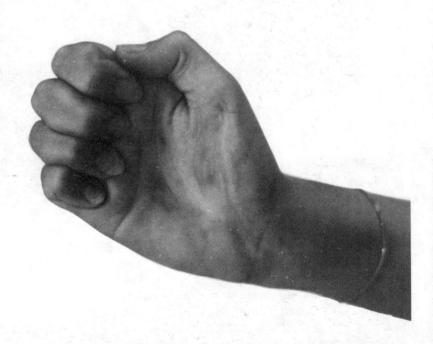

The Fist

A fisted hand can deliver a great deal of power when the punch is executed properly. The fist must be properly formed in order to eliminate possible damage to the hand when making contact. The thumb is wrapped around the outside of the fingers for two purposes: to eliminate injury to the thumb when contact is made, and to reinforce the "tightness" of the striking fist. Other variations of the fist are the straight knuckle and extended knuckle formation.

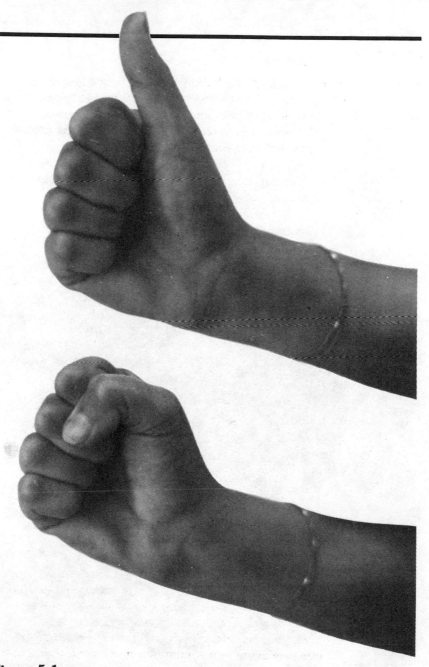

Figure 5.1
*The thumb is wrapped around the outside of the
fingers when forming a fist.*

Punching

The focal point of a punch should be the face or the abdomen. The shortest distance between two points is a straight line. Consider your fist to be point A, and the assailant's face or abdomen to be point B. The trajectory or flight of the punching action is linear. Actual fist contact is made off of the first two or three knuckles, depending upon the size of your hand. Keep your wrist tense and straight.

Figure 5.2   *Front and side view.*

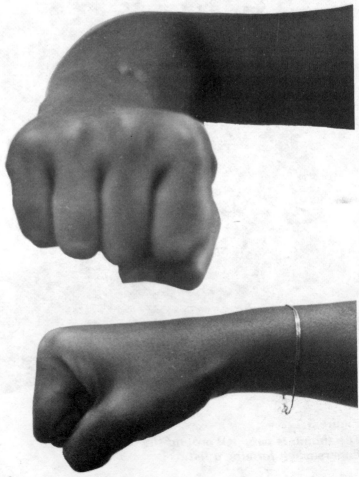

Hip rotation is an important source of power in punch delivery. When considering the comparable strength and size of an assailant and the victim, the assailant is generally at an advantage. Unless the assailant is caught totally off guard, power exerted strictly from the victim's upper body is not enough to ward off the assailant.

Figure 5.3   *The straight knuckle formation.*

Figure 5.4   *The extended knuckle formation.*

In a solid stance the hips are slightly tilted and the fist is drawn back to the waist. The hips are the initiator of power. The first movement occurs in the hips as they rotate in a forward action which gives the upper body additional power.

Palm Attacks

There are many similarities between a punch and a palm attack. The only consequential difference between the two is the hand position. In the palm attack the fingers are drawn back to touch the pads of the hand (similar to the first photo in figure 5.1). The palm of the hand is extended and tension is exerted in the wrist. The contact area is the base of the palm.

Figure 5.5
The palm is used to attack under the nose in an upward motion.

Trajectory. The trajectory of the straight punch and the palm attack is from low to high in a linear motion. The closer the attacking hand can be brought back to the waist, in conjunction with the rotation of the hips, the more powerful the attack will be.

The palm attack can also be used to attack under the chin, again in an upward trajectory. In this manner the head is jolted back and leaves the vulnerable throat region exposed.

Figure 5.6
The palm is used to attack under the chin in an upward motion which exposes the throat.

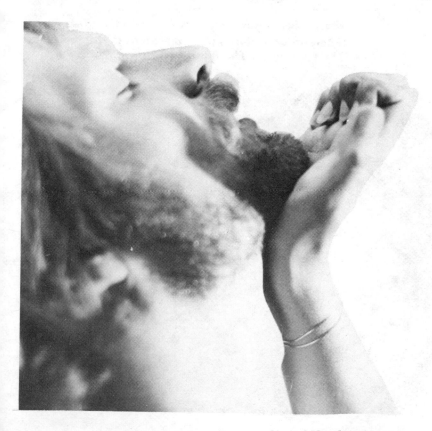

The Ridgehand

The inside portion of the hand is utilized as the striking point in the ridgehand. The trajectory of the ridgehand is similar to that of the punch; however, a snapping action from the hips causes a slightly rounded and whipping action. Target areas for the ridgehand are the temples and the base of the skull.

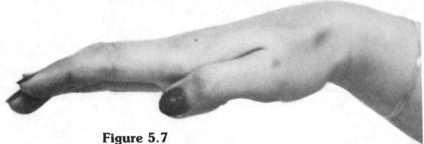

Figure 5.7
The contact area of the ridgehand is the inside of the forefinger. The hand is held rigid.

Figure 5.8
The ridgehand can be used to strike the temple.

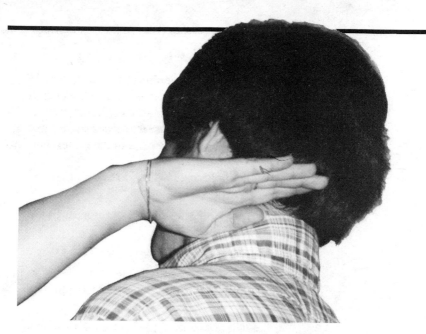

Figure 5.9
The base of the skull is a vulnerable target area.

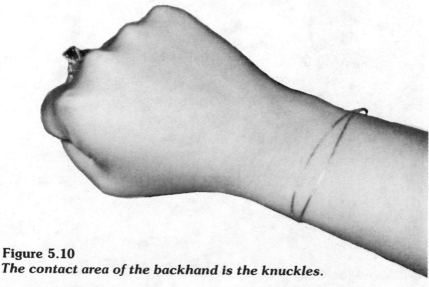

Figure 5.10
The contact area of the backhand is the knuckles.

The Backhand

The backhand is another variation of a hand attack. The hand is held in a fisted position perpendicular to the target, rather than parallel to it as the punch is. Generally, the backhand is used to strike the temple area. The size of the fisted hand is much larger than the temple area.

To execute the backhand the following motions should be performed:

1. The striking hand is in a fisted position, with the wrist straight.

2. Think of the elbow as a pivotal point.

3. As the striking motion begins, tense the muscles in the forearm and wrist, making contact with the knuckles.

4. Withdraw the backhand as quickly as possible.

Figure 5.11
The backhand is used to strike the temple.

Finger Attacks

Using the hands—particularly the fingers—to attack the eyes is a highly effective self-defense technique. However, many people may be uncomfortable using this method. Because gouging becomes a programmed or learned response for most people, self-defense instructors are debating whether or not to teach it.

The similarities among gouging and scratching techniques are as follows:

Figure 5.12
The eye gouge follows the same low to high trajectory of the punch or palm attack.

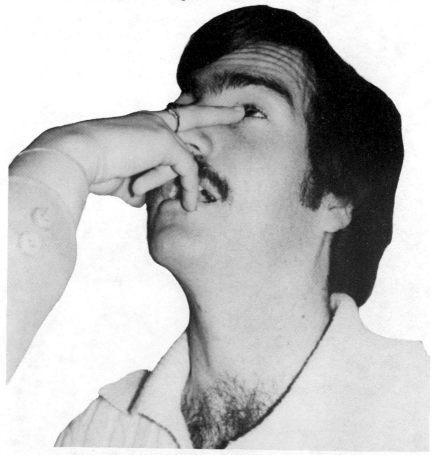

Gouging. The fingers are extended outward in this attack. The low to high trajectory of the strike is similar to that of the palm attack and the straight punch.

This trajectory is more effective than the high to low trajectory which is "telegraphed" in advance and thus, easily blocked. Keeping in a low to high position, contact can be made below the eyes and pushed upward.

Figure 5.13
The two-finger gouge below eyes.

Scratching. Fingernails are a natural weapon. The facial region is the primary target area. A scratching attack has a two-fold purpose: (1) injury to the face (particularly the eyes), and (2) a means of providing an identification mark on the assailant. In reporting the attack, tell the police where the scratch marks were made. Segments of the assailant's skin may be under your nails. This, too, should be drawn to the attention of the police. An identifiable scratch mark or specimen of skin may lead to apprehension of the assailant.

Figure 5.14
Due to height difference, the assailant is scratched in a straight downward action.

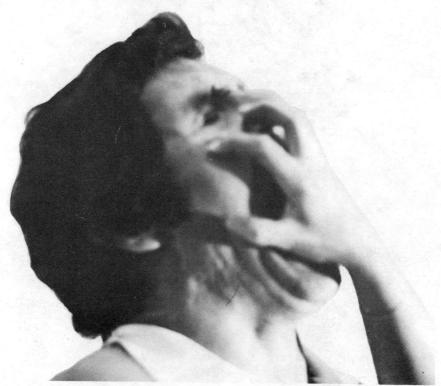

Scratching is one of the few techniques where you use either a straight high to low or a diagonal high to low trajectory with the striking hand. It is extremely difficult to use a low to high trajectory due to close proximity and hand position.

Figure 5.15
Scratching with diagonal trajectory.

Pulling

The head area has two areas vulnerable to a pulling action, the hair and the ears. Since close proximity is necessary to accomplish this, some type of simultaneous lower body attack should be executed. You must have a firm hold when pulling the hair. The area adjacent to the temple region is more sensitive than other areas of the head. In executing a hair pull, face the assailant, firmly grab a large handful of hair on each side if possible; if long, wrap it around your hand and pull in a down and outward direction. This usually causes the assailant's body to bend forward, facilitating a quickly delivered knee attack.

Figure 5.16
Pull the hair in a down and outward direction.

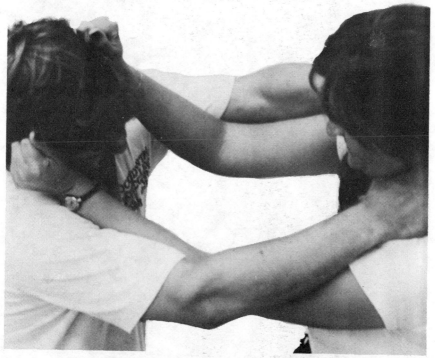

Attacks to the Throat

The throat is another vulnerable area which is usually exposed and accessible. Striking to the throat will—at the very minimum—cause the assailant to gag and hesitate, which allows the victim to proceed with another attack. As with the other hand attacks, a low to high trajectory is best.

Figure 5.17
The knuckles are used to attack to the throat.

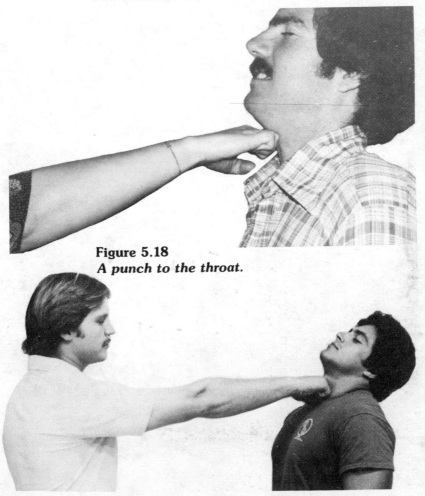

Figure 5.18
A punch to the throat.

Figure 5.19
The fingers (Spear-hand) to the throat.

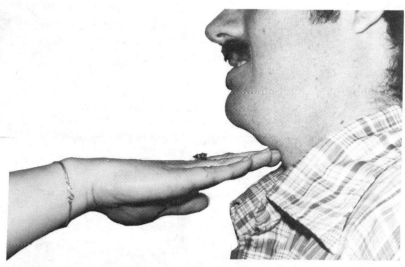

Figure 5.20
Since the "Adam's apple" is generally pronounced, it can be grabbed easily.

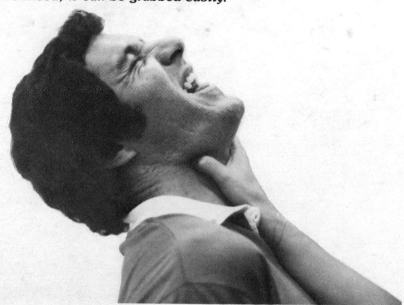

ELBOW ATTACKS

Elbow attacks are used when there is close proximity between the victim and the assailant. Elbow range is restricted compared to leg and arm range. However, when close proximity has been set, the elbow can be a highly effective weapon. Variations of the elbow attack can be used to defend against a frontal attack, a rear attack, and a side attack. The elbow is a bony structure, and thus is—innately—an effective weapon. If you can use hip rotation in the direction of the attack, the power of the hip thrust, in addition to the elbow, will maximize its effectiveness.

Figure 5.21
In a proper side elbow attack the hips are parallel to the ground.

Correct

All elbow attacks share these similarities:

1. The elbow is the striking implement.

2. When delivering an elbow attack the hips and elbows should be as parallel to the ground as possible. Leaning in the direction of the elbow causes instability and loss of balance.

3. The body weight is lowered so that a stable stance is accomplished. Lifting up onto the toes generally causes loss of balance and power.

Figure 5.22
Leaning in the direction of the elbow will will make you lose power.

Incorrect

Front Elbow Attacks

Front elbow attacks can be used to attack under the chin. When possible, use the thrust of the hip in the same direction of the elbow attack. The head of the assailant will jerk back, leaving the highly vulnerable throat area exposed. The front elbow attack should be noted as a technique that works well even when an extreme height difference between the assailant and the would-be victim exists. Since the contact point is the chin and the striking implement is the elbow, an appreciable height difference can exist while losing little power.

When delivering the front elbow strike:

1. Clench the fist of the striking arm so that tension exists throughout the arm.

2. As the striking action occurs, draw the clenched fist past the ear.

3. Withdraw the elbow and strike any vulnerable, exposed area.

Figure 5.23
The front elbow is used to attack under the chin. Note the close proximity of the victim and assailant.

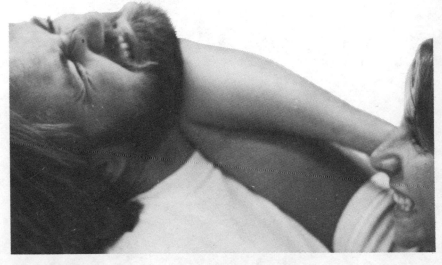

Side Elbow Attacks

Side elbow strikes are used in assaults to the side of the body. The attack is usually reserved for striking the solar plexus. Again, elbow attacks should not be attempted unless close proximity exists.

To execute a side elbow strike:

1. Elevate the hand and forearm to approximately chest height.

2. Clench the fist in a palm-up position.

3. Slide the arm toward striking target while rotating your fist to palm-down position.

4. Maintain balance by keeping the upper body perpendicular to floor with weight distributed equally. Avoid leaning.

5. Think of the upper arm and lower arm as one unit. Move the unit as a whole.

Figure 5.24
The side elbow is used to attack the solar plexus.

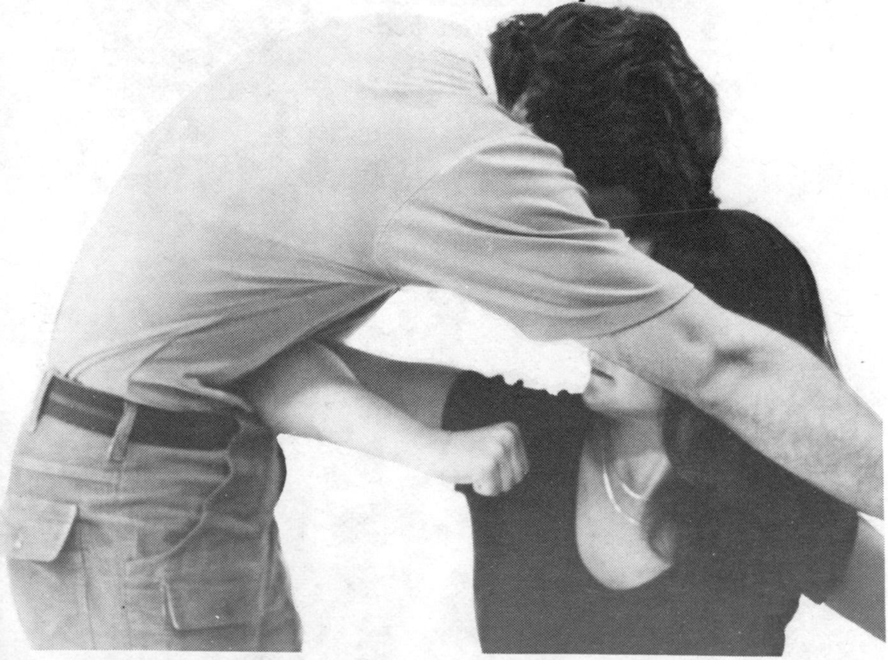

Back Elbow Attacks

The back elbow strike is used when being attacked from the rear. The movement of the back elbow strike resembles those preparatory movements of a straight punch. When executing the punch the fisted hand is drawn back to the waist. At this point the palm is facing upward. In essence these are the same movements of a back elbow attack. The target area is generally the solar plexus, or if there is an extreme height difference, the groin. The back elbow attack can and should be used in conjunction with other attacks.

When executing the back elbow strike the following motions should be performed:

1. Rotate the hips slightly in order to allow the target area to become open.

2. Slide the elbow quickly and with strength when this opening occurs.

Figure 5.25
The back elbow attack is used when approached from the rear.

Figure 5.26
The back elbow attack with stomping kick.

6

DEFENSIVE MOVEMENTS

Defensive movements are *protective* in nature. Blocking a punch or a bludgeon is a defensive movement. Generally speaking, in a spontaneous assault a defensive movement is necessary before an offensive or counterattack movement can take place. Naturally, one of the best defensive measures is simply not to be there. However, many times this is not an option.

In defensive movements the individual must often decide on a trade-off. For example, an assailant is about to strike you with a crowbar. It is obvious that your head is the intended target. Being self-defense conscious you realize that you must protect your head. By blocking your head there is a realistic possibility that the crowbar will strike you in the back. This is a trade-off decision you must make instantaneously.

The four defensive blocks we will discuss are: the cross block, the head block, the middle block and the kick defense.

CROSS BLOCK

The cross block is used when being accosted with either an overhead or kicking motion. The overhead cross block is used when being attacked in any overhead motion, whether it is a bludgeon (i.e. crowbar) or a punch. The kick cross block is used in defense of any kicking motion.

To execute the cross block:

1. Cross fisted hands at the wrist, perpendicular to the floor.

2. Thrust the cross block toward striking object.

Figure 6.1
The overhead cross block is used when being attacked by an overhead motion.

3. In blocking the upper body, special attention should be taken so that the head and facial areas are out of the range of contact.

Disadvantage. Although the cross block is considered to be a strong block, there is an innate weakness in its execution. The disadvantage lies in the fact that both hands are involved in the blocking action. Special consideration should be taken to recover quickly from the defensive action, so that an offensive or counteracting motion can take place.

Figure 6.2
The kick cross block should be aimed at the lower leg.

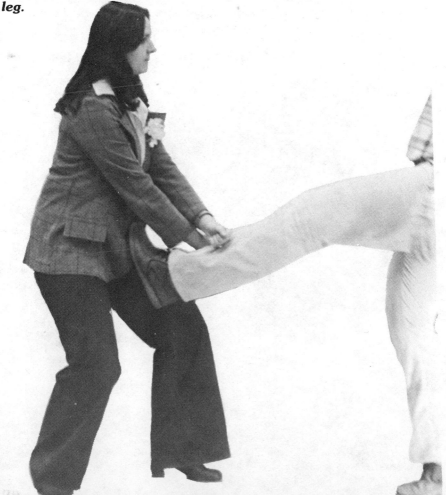

ONE ARM BLOCKS
Head Block

The one arm head block is used to defend against overhead or face assaults. Although less power is generated in the head block than in the cross block, there are marked advantages (depending upon the particular situations). These advantages are: one arm is generally enough to deflect the strike, and the non-blocking hand and arm can be used concurrently in an offensive or attacking motion.

When executing the head block the following motions should be performed:

Figure 6.3
The head block in starting and ending positions.

1. The forearm of the blocking arm rotates in a counterclockwise motion as the arm is raised to the forehead.

2. The elbow is kept bent.

3. Blocking contact is made with the outside edge of the lower forearm.

4. The actual blocking point is determined by the situation. However, blocking slightly above the forehead generally insures that the striking implement or fist will be deflected.

5. Withdraw the block arm and counterattack.

Figure 6.4
The head block can be used when being struck in an overhead motion.

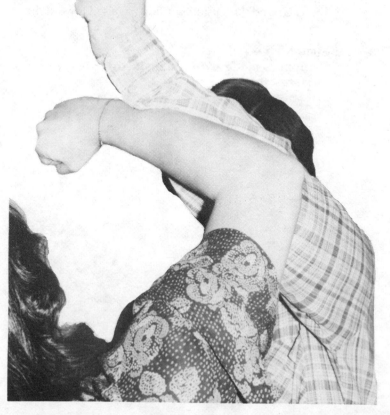

Middle Blocks

Middle blocks are used to block and deflect attacks between the neck and waist. There are two basic blocks, the inside block and the outside block. The name of the block indicates its direction. The inside block moves toward the midline of the body, while the outside block moves toward the outside of the body. Again, each individual has preferential movements and utilization of either block is a matter of choice.

Inside Block. The contact area of this particular block is the inside of the lower forearm. The particular level of the assailant's attack will cause variation in the execution of the block.

When executing the inside block the following points should be noted:

1. The hand, in a fisted position, is raised toward the ear.

Figure 6.5
Contact is made with the inside of the forearm.

Figure 6.6
The inside block progression.

2. The fist remains perpendicular to the ground with the elbow high.

3. The wrist is kept straight.

4. The block is executed in a sweeping motion *toward* the midline of the body.

5. The fist remains above the elbow.

6. Contact is made with the inside of the lower forearm of the blocking arm.

   Special Considerations. The across the body movement of the inside block can "close up" the vulnerable areas of the assailant's body, and thus, limits your counterattack possibilities.

Figure 6.7
The outside block contact area is the outside of the forearm.

Outside Block. The outside block differs from the inside block only in direction. When executing the outside block:

1. The hand is in a fisted position with the palm facing down; the elbow is in a bent position with the forearm extended across the body.

2. The elbow is approximately a fist length away from the side.

3. The block is executed in a sweeping motion *away from* the midline of the body.

4. The blocking motion is as parallel to the ground as possible to protect the greatest amount of area.

Special Considerations. Due to the follow-through motion of the outside block, areas of the assailant's mid-section tend to become open, thereby increasing the possible areas of counterattack. Although this is a benefit of the block, the complete motion of the block is slightly more difficult to execute.

Figure 6.8
The outside block progression.

Kick Defense

This defense is used in blocking or deflecting kicks. Since there is usually distance between the assailant and would-be victim when a kick is executed, a viable option is to move out of the way. Many times this is not possible due to the speed of delivery. Blocking the kick can be hazardous because of the amount of force which can be exerted in kicking. The kick defense is actually a deflecting motion. As with other defensive moves, the blocking is a sweeping action.

Figure 6.9
The kick defense is used to deflect a kick.

To execute the kick defense:

1. The blocking hand should be in a fisted position with the fist raised to the outside of the body.

2. The elbow is flexed.

3. Strike downward in a sweeping motion, deflecting the kick.

4. Keep the upper body perpendicular to the floor and the body weight low in order to prevent loss of balance.

5. Contact is made with the outside of the lower forearm with palm facing downward.

Figure 6.10
Kick defense progression.

RELEASES

Releases are tactics which free the individual from immediate contact. The term release is a technical term for an escape from a hold—they are not intended to harm the assailant. It is important to keep this in mind since spontaneous counterattacking is necessary. Although releasing yourself from immediate contact is the first step in defending yourself, it must be accompanied by an offensive or attacking movement. Keep in mind—releases cause no harm!

This chapter will examine wrist releases, front choke holds and bear hugs.

WRIST RELEASE

The hand is the most natural implement for grasping. If you grab for a wrist, note how the fingers and thumb encircle the wrist. By tightening the muscles in the hand the grasp becomes firm. The thumb is one of the weakest parts of the body, with very little action except for this grasping action. If an assailant were to grab at your wrist, his hand would probably encircle your wrist firmly. It is necessary to play upon the weakest point of this encasement, the thumb. To break a wrist grab move your wrist in the direction the assailant's thumb points.

Figure 7.1
The wrist should be moved in the direction the assailant's thumb points.

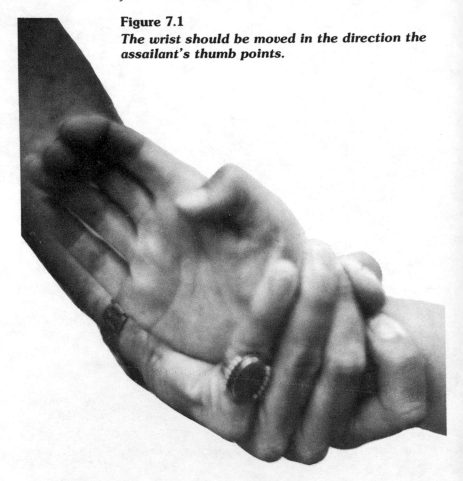

If you were grabbed while walking down the street your first reaction would probably be to pull away. This is natural, and a self-defense conscious person should recognize it as such. After the initial reaction you must take the situation in hand and execute a release.

An important consideration to keep in mind in any situation requiring a release is the time factor. An individual is grabbed for a reason. The grab will inevitably be followed by other motions. Therefore, the would-be victim needs to act quickly.

The Single-Handed Release

A single-handed release is one where one hand is involved. Due to the quickness needed in the execution of the release the following steps should be executed simultaneously:

1. Drop your elbow.
2. Lower your body weight.
3. Slide your wrist in direction of assailant's thumb.

Figure 7.2
Progression of the single-hand wrist release.

Remember: no matter how the wrist is grabbed, the principle is the same; the smallest portion of the wrist comes out of the weakest portion of the grip, in this case the thumb.

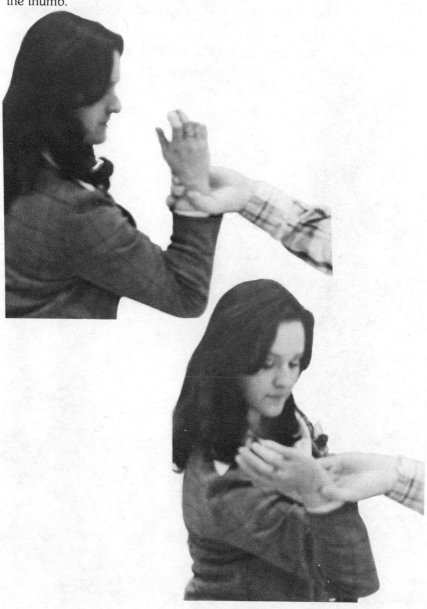

The Two-Handed Release

Releases are two-handed when both hands of the assailant and/or the victim are involved. The principle is the same as that of the single-handed release. Since the

Figure 7.3
Progression of the two-handed release.

thumb is the weakest portion of the grip, you must take advantage of it. Keep in mind that a release will not injure the assailant; therefore the release must be immediately followed by an attacking move.

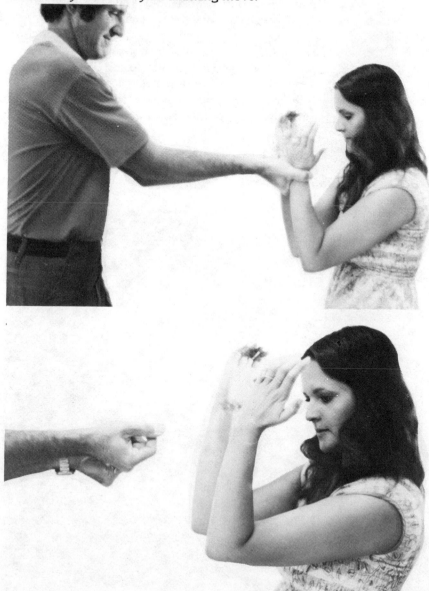

FRONT CHOKE HOLD

The front choke hold is one of the most common assaults. Generally some type of attack has preceded and has resulted in a choke hold. The most important factor to consider in any type of choke hold is that maintenance of an oxygen flow is vital, and is your chief concern. Any type of choke or strangulation hold limits the oxygen flow and can ultimately cost you your life. The self-defense conscious individual is aware of this and should react by immediately dropping the chin and pulling it inward, thereby allowing the air exchange to take place.

Figure 7.4
The chin should be dropped in order to allow air flow.

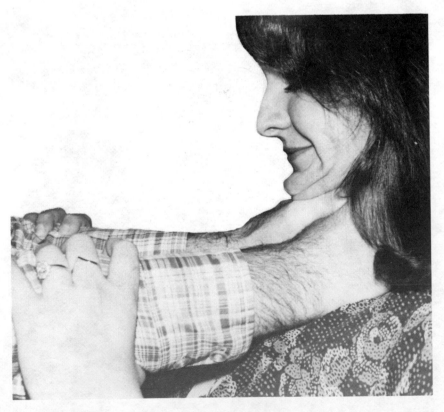

Choke holds leave the victim a variety of variables to consider (such as height and strength differences between assailant and victim, the amount of struggle prior to the choke hold, etc.) so that no one specific release is best. Usually the hand attacks, particularly those to the throat or eyes, are appropriate. The assailant must be incapacitated.

Figure 7.5
Bear hug with an elbow attack.

BEAR HUG

The bear hug is another fairly common hold which, unlike the front choke hold, is usually a spontaneous attack. Again, in each situation, there are a variety of variables to be considered. In situations where the height and strength differences are not insurmountable, elbow

Figure 7.6
The elbow attack, stomping kick and head smash should be executed as simultaneously as possible.

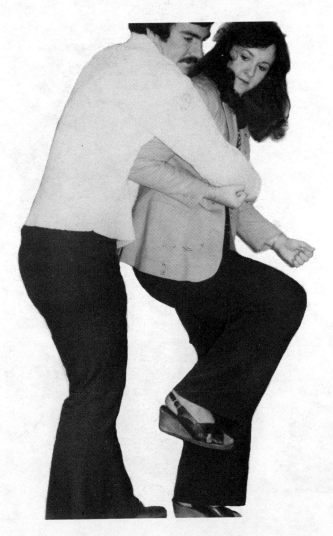

and/or stomping kicks in conjunction with a head smash are suggested. The head smash is executed by smashing the back of the head into the face of the assailant. The occipital area of the head is extremely hard, and the face extremely vulnerable. The attack and/or stomping kick will cause the assailant to react by bending forward, which draws the face forward and into target range.

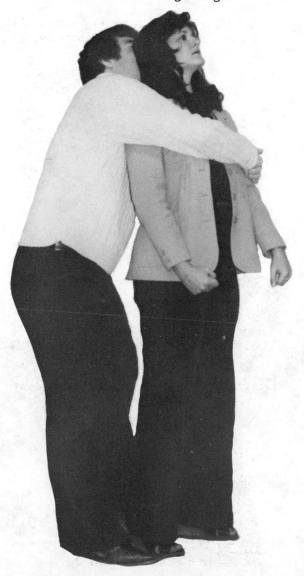

LOSING THE FIRST ROUND

I n this chapter we will examine two types of instances which constitute the victim "losing the first round." The first is the situation where the assailant has grounded (driven to the ground) the victim and the second is where the victim is assaulted while lying on the ground.

GROUND RECOVERY

In many spontaneous assaults the assailant has an advantage in the element of surprise. Under some circumstances even the self-defense conscious individual can be overtaken without warning. When the assailant has the advantage it is of prime importance that the victim recover from the fall, move out of the assailant's range and assume a defensive ground stance. This can be accomplished by rolling onto the side of the body and out of the way of the assailant. There is a high probability that the assailant will move in his intended victim's direction, therefore it is vital that the recovery is quick.

GROUND POSITION

The defensive ground position can be assumed by quickly rolling over and rising to the knees while sitting on the heels. The upper body weight is slightly forward.

Although this may appear to be a vulnerable position, it is quite functional and allows optimal defensive movements. If rushed by the assailant, the

Figure 8.1
The ground position on the knees.

would-be victim is both in a balanced and braced position. The most important consideration is positioning. The would-be victim is below the assailant, which is an added advantage. If the assailant lunges forward to strike with his upper extremities, he must use a downward trajectory which places him in an unbalanced position. If the assailant attempts to kick, the kick can be blocked using the same kick defense previously discussed in Chapter Six. However, a defensive stance in an upright position is always preferable to the grounded defensive stance.

Figure 8.2
The ground kick defense is similar to the upright kick defense.

SUPINE ATTACK

The second type of assault can occur under two conditions. In the first situation the would-be victim is supine and sees the assailant. If this occurs, kick to the groin and scream.

Figure 8.3
Kick to the groin and scream.

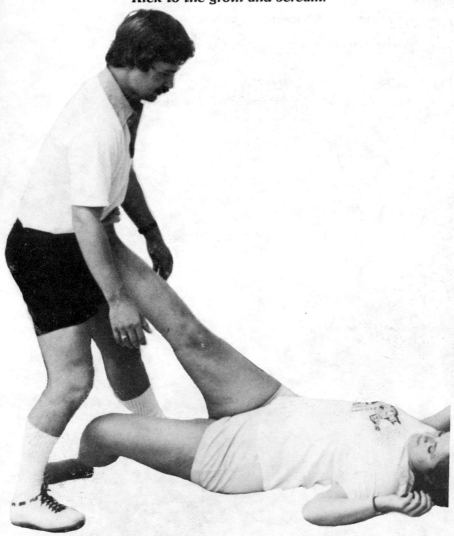

If the assailant has begun to jump on top of you, his momentum is going in a forward direction. Use this momentum to execute the following technique:

1. Push the dominant foot into the assailant's midsection or groin while grabbing the upper body clothing.

Figure 8.4
Use the momentum of the assailant to your advantage.

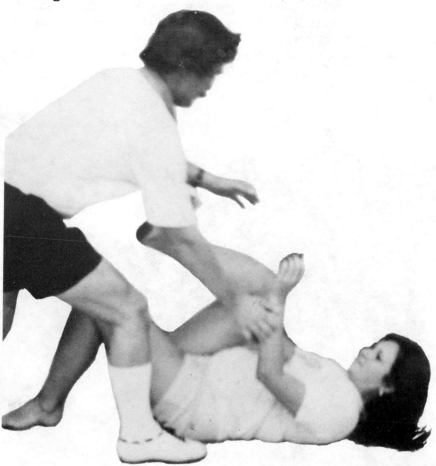

2. Forcefully extend your dominant leg to momentarily support the assailant's weight.

3. Lift the hips and vigorously push the assailant up and over your head.

4. Roll onto your side and assume a grounded defensive stance, or quickly jump up and run away, if possible, or attack with kicks to the assailant's face.

Assaults in a supine position are as diverse and situational as any other spontaneous attack, therefore the self-defense conscious individual should incorporate any defense which is needed. This includes *eye attacks*, throat attacks or scratching. Remember the assailant is not playing by any rules! Losing the first round does *not* mean losing the battle!

FITNESS AND PRACTICE

P ERSONAL FITNESS

In developing self-defense consciousness you must understand the relationship between personal fitness and personal defense. Your fitness could be a deciding factor in the success or failure of a threatening encounter. Strength and endurance are recurring factors in self-defense training. In some cases flexibility and agility can be added. It has been pointed out that each individual needs to recognize and refine preferential or natural movements. Some strength and endurance is achieved through the refining process, however overall fitness contributes to both the refining process and your strength. Your fitness program should encompass two aspects of fitness: (1) overall fitness and (2) specific fitness. Overall fitness encompasses endurance building activities and specific fitness develops strength and flexibility.

Overall Fitness

Running and skipping rope are excellent means of maintaining cardiovascular endurance and leg strength.

Running. When running, begin by covering a short distance in a moderate time. Gradually increase either the distance covered in the same time (thereby increasing your running pace) or both time and distance covered.

The defense-conscious person is well aware that running away from a threatening situation is a viable solution to the problem.

Figure 9.1
Running provides overall fitness.

Jumping Rope. Jumping rope is another inexpensive way of building endurance. Jumping rope also adds to coordination. A suggested way to build endurance through jumping rope is to jump for increasing time periods. Start with one minute and work toward five, and then ten.

Warming Up. Prior to any exercise, a few minutes should be spent warming up the body. Slow stretching exercises are excellent. Avoid bouncing and jerking motions until after the body is warmed up. Slow warm-up exercises minimize the likelihood of injuries.

Figure 9.2
Jumping rope.

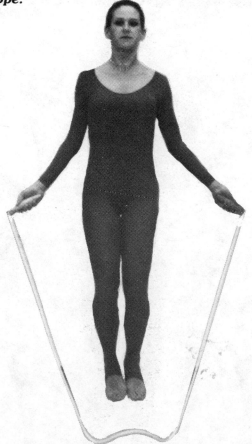

Specific Fitness

Torso Twist. Stand with your feet apart and arms outstretched. Twist the torso from side to side. Repeat 25 times on each side.

Figure 9.3
Torso twist.

Toe Touches. Stand with your feet apart and arms outstretched. Touch your right foot with your left hand, and straighten up, then touch your left foot with your right hand and straighten up. Repeat 50 times, alternating sides.

Figure 9.4
Toe touches.

Torso Stretch. In a sitting position with the legs spread apart and arms outstretched, reach for one foot with palm turned up, return to starting position, and stretch to the opposite side. Repeat 20 times on each side.

Figure 9.5
Torso stretch.

Side Leg Raises. Lie on your right side, head resting on right arm which is extended beyond head on the floor. Keep your legs straight with the left leg on top of the right. Lift the left leg upward. Lower leg to starting position. Repeat to a 20 count, then roll onto opposite side and repeat.

Figure 9.6
Side leg raises.

Push-Ups. This exercise strengthens the arms, shoulders, neck and back. Lie face down with the palms of your hands on the floor. Push against the floor until your arms are straight. Your body should be kept straight.

Figure 9.7
Push-ups.

PRACTICE AIDS

Unlike many activities, the physical dimension of self-defense is difficult to practice. The mechanics of the various strikes, blows and kicks can and should be practiced, however, without a partner and feedback, force and accuracy are difficult to achieve. In order to achieve competency, targets should be substituted as practice aids. In practicing attacks, the following equipment can be effectively used.

Balls. Volleyball, playground, or soccer balls can be used to practice face attacks. Masking tape can be used to mark eye and nose "targets." Have a friend hold up the ball and practice facial attacks. Dipping your fingers and hands in chalk and then striking will give you an indication of accuracy.

Figure 9.8
An "X" marks the vital spots in this eye attack.

Punching Bags. Punching bags can be used in much the same manner as balls. The advantage is that a partner is not needed. If practicing punches, mark the facial area and solar plexus. Tackling dummies, a rolled exercise mat, padded posts, a sofa or chair cushions can be used interchangeably to practice the most basic skills. Use masking tape to mark the targets. Practice accurate and forceful strikes. If used to practice kicks, mark knee and groin targets. If using a padded post or padded wall, make sure the padding is thick and in good condition to avoid injury.

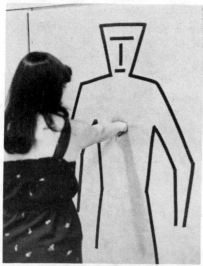

Figure 9.9
Punch to the solar plexus.

Figure 9.10
Kick to the groin.

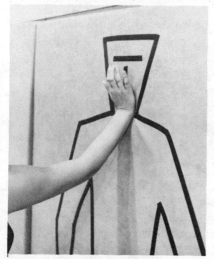

Figure 9.11
Palm attack to the chin.

Figure 9.12
Punch to the nose

Blocking Pads. Blocking pads make excellent aids in practicing punches and kicks. A partner should be used to hold the pad in place. The partner bracing the pad should maintain a solid stance.

Figure 9.13
Blocking pads can be used to practice punching.

Figure 9.14
Blocking pads can be adjusted to practice kicks.

SUGGESTED READINGS

Pirnat, J. *Personal Defense Skills.*
Champaign, IL: Stipes Publishing Co., 1975.
Sylvain, G. *Defense and Control Tactics.*
Englewood Cliffs, NJ: Prentice-Hall, Inc., 1971.
Wyness, G. *Practical Personal Defense.*
Palo Alto, CA: Mayfield Publishing Co., 1975.
Sheffield, Emilyn. *Total Fitness For Women.*
Santa Monica: Goodyear Publishing Company, Inc., 1980.

HOW TO USE THE EVALUATION FORMS

The forms which follow were designed to be used in a variety of instructional settings. Pre-planning and organization are necessary for these devices to be used as effectively as possible. The purpose of evaluation is to gauge how well the course objectives are accomplished. That is, evaluation will indicate the progress and the extent to which the learning has occurred.

Although the learner must do his own learning, the instructor's role is to guide and direct learning experiences, and to provide for appropriate measurement procedures. The charts which follow have been constructed to place primary responsibility on the learner for estimating progress and indicating areas that need work. It may not be necessary or desirable to use all the materials provided here in certain teaching-learning situations. The instructor and the student should work together to select the materials most appropriate for their work.

Sufficient time for practice and study must be provided if the individual is to perfect her skills and develop understanding. The time available may not be adequate for *all* students to demonstrate acceptable levels of skill performance.

PERSONAL SAFETY

NAME_____ DATE_____

	YES	NO

At home do you . . .

- have a peephole in your door?

- have your name listed by first initial and last name?

- have a deadbolt lock?

- keep your shades drawn at night?

- have an unlisted phone number?

When walking do you . . .
- walk with confidence?

- stay in well-lighted areas?

- dress appropriately?

- keep personal belongings clutched closely to you?

When driving in a car do you . . .
- always check the back seat before entering?

- keep windows rolled up at night?

- make sure doors are kept locked?

- always park in well-lighted areas?

- avoid traveling to new places at night?

BASIC SKILLS

NAME_____   **DATE**_____

STANCE

	Good	Fair	Poor

- Knees are slightly flexed

- One foot is in front of the other

- Weight is distributed slightly forward on toes

- Arms are flexed with hands clenched

KICKS

Front Kick

- Supporting leg is flexed

- Weight is distributed equally between toes and heel of supporting leg

- Knee of kicking leg is raised high

- Ball of foot is extended

- Leg is fully extended in kicking motion

- Contact is made with ball of foot

Side Kick

- Supporting leg is flexed

- Weight is distributed equally between toes and heel of supporting leg

- Knee of kicking leg is raised high

- Toes of kicking foot face forward

- Heel is slightly extended

- Kicking leg is thrust to target

- Contact is made with side of foot

Stomping Kick

- Supporting leg is flexed
- Weight is distributed equally between toes and heel of supporting leg
- Knee of kicking leg is raised high

- Heel of kicking foot is thrust downward
- Weight is transferred onto stomping heel as supporting leg is straightened

BASIC SKILLS

NAME_____ DATE_____

HAND ATTACKS

Palm Attacks	Good	Fair	Poor

Palm Attacks

- Fingers are drawn back to touch pads of hands _____
- Palm of hand is extended _____
- Tension is exerted in wrist _____
- Palm is thrust forward _____
- Contact is made with heel of palm _____

Backhand

- Hand is in fisted position _____
- Wrist is straight and tense _____
- Backhand is perpendicular to target _____
- Elbow is used as pivotal point _____
- Backhand is snapped to target area _____
- Contact is made with knuckles _____
- Hand is withdrawn quickly _____

BASIC SKILLS

NAME_____   DATE_____

ELBOW ATTACKS

	Good	Fair	Poor

Front Elbow

- Fist of striking arm is clenched

- Tension is exerted throughout arm

- Arm is flexed at elbow

- As strike occurs, clenched fist is drawn past ear

- Contact is made with elbow

Side Elbow

- Hand and forearm are elevated to chest height

- Fist is clenched in palm-up position

- Slide arm toward target while rotating fist to palm-down position

- Body remains perpendicular to floor

- Contact is made with elbow

Back Elbow

- Fist of striking arm is clenched

- Fisted hand is brought to waist height

- Arm is flexed at elbow

- Elbow is thrust backward to target

- Hips rotate as thrust occurs, thereby opening target

- Contact is made with elbow

DEFENSIVE MOVEMENTS

NAME_____ DATE_____

DEFENSIVE MOVEMENTS

	Good	Fair	Poor

Cross Block

- Fisted hands are crossed at wrist

- Wrists are tense and straight

- Block is thrust toward striking object

- Weight is distributed in a slightly forward direction with knees forward

Head Block

- Fist of blocking arm is clenched

- Forearm of blocking arm rotates in counterclockwise motion as the arm is raised to the forehead

- Elbow is bent

- Blocking contact is made with outside edge of the lower forearm

Inside Middle Block

- Fist of blocking arm is clenched

- Fisted hand is raised toward ear

- Wrist is straight

- Sweeping motion occurs toward midline of body

- Contact is made with the inside of the lower forearm

Outside Middle Block

- Fist of blocking arm is clenched

- Elbow is in bent position with forearm facing upward

- Wrist is straight
- Sweeping motion occurs away from the midline of the body
- Contact is made with the outside of the lower forearm

Kick Defense

- Fist of blocking arm is clenched

- Fist is raised to outside of body

- Elbow is flexed

- Strike downward in sweeping motion

- Contact is made with outside of the lower forearm
- Upper body remains perpendicular to floor

TEST YOUR KNOWLEDGE

I. True—False
    If the statement is TRUE, place a "T" in the blank.
    If the statement is FALSE, place an "F" in the blank.

_____ 1. The ability to recognize and avoid a possible threatening situation is a preparedness component of self defense.

_____ 2. Reflexive movements are always learned.

_____ 3. It is wise to stop for a motorist on the highway if emergency lights are flashing.

_____ 4. A rapist's main objective is usually sexual satisfaction.

_____ 5. Spontaneous attacks are those which occur without forewarning.

_____ 6. The source of power in delivering a kick is the upper leg.

_____ 7. When executing a hand attack, you should lean in the direction of the strike to gain greater distance.

_____ 8. Facial attacks should always be executed from a high to low motion.

_____ 9. Psychological readiness is the ability to analyze a situation and respond effectively.

_____ 10. If stopped by a law enforcement officer in an unmarked car, it is wise to ask for identification.

_____ 11. It is wise to run away from all threatening situations.

_____ 12. Making eye contact with an assailant may give you a psychological edge.

_____ 13. Gouging and scratching techniques are similar in motion.

_____ 14. All assailants must be physically dealt with.

_____ 15. The dominant target area for the stomping kick is the knee.

_____ 16. The kick defensive is a solid block to the assailant's leg.

_____ 17. A cross block is the most advantageous block to employ due to its strength.

_____ 18. A release is a tactic used to free yourself as well as impart pain to the assailant.

_____ 19. All attacks are spontaneous.

_____ 20. The outside and inside middle block differ only in direction.

II. Multiple Choice

Circle the letter by the most correct statement.

21. When listing your phone number in a directory, list
    a. a false name and inform your friends
    b. first and last names
    c. first initial and last name
22. Which of the following is NOT an offensive movement.
    a. Palm attack to the chin
    b. Front kick to the groin
    c. Overhead cross block
    d. Punch to the face
23. In which kick does a weight transfer occur?
    a. Front kick
    b. Stomping kick
    c. Side kick
24. Which of the following is NOT a home precaution for living in an apartment?
    a. Install a peephole to view visitors
    b. Make duplicate keys for "good" friends only
    c. List your name on the building directory with only the first initial and last name
    d. Change the lock on the door when moving in
25. Which set of movements are likely to share the same trajectory?
    a. Punch and palm attack
    b. Front kick and side kick
    c. Side elbow and front elbow
26. The greatest distance is usually covered in the
    a. Side kick
    b. Punch
    c. Front kick
27. Which is not an advantage of the defensive ground stance?
    a. A kick from the assailant can be readily blocked
    b. A braced position in case you are rushed
    c. Allows a great deal of ground movement

III. Fill in the answer to each question.

28. What are the three dimensions of self-defense?

   a. _____

   b. _____

   c. _____

29. Since each individual possesses preferential movement patterns, each must

   a. _____

   b. _____

30. Name four facial target areas.

   a. _____

   b. _____

   c. _____

   d. _____

31. An individual faced with possible rape has three options. Name them.

   a. _____

   b. _____

   c. _____

32. The two dominant contact areas for the front kick are:

   a. _____

   b. _____

33. Name the most common target area for the following elbow attacks:

   a. front elbow attack _____

   b. side elbow attack_____

   c. back elbow attack _____

34. Middle blocks are utilized to block or defect attacks between what two body areas?

   a. _____

   b. _____

35. Name four body parts which are effective weapons:

   a. _____

   b. _____

   c. _____

   d. _____

Possible score: 50   Score: _____